ABC Coloring Book Uppercase Letters

Copyright © 2020 Sharon Asher

All rights reserved.

No part of this book may be copied and/or altered and/or distributed and/or reproduced in any form or by any electronic or mechanical means, including but not limited to information storage and retrieval systems, without express permission in writing from the author.

ISBN-13: 978-1-951462-05-5

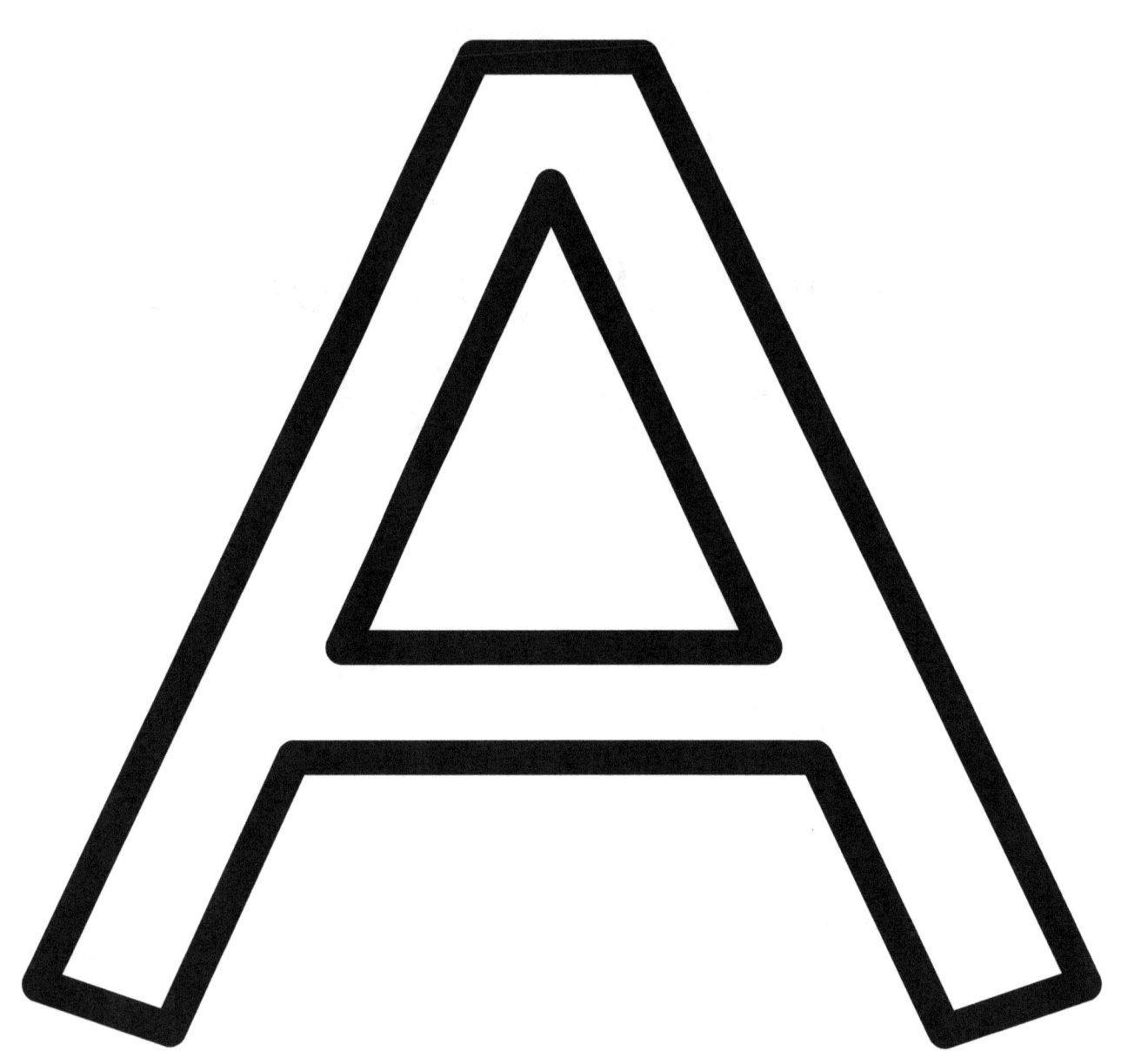

Acorn

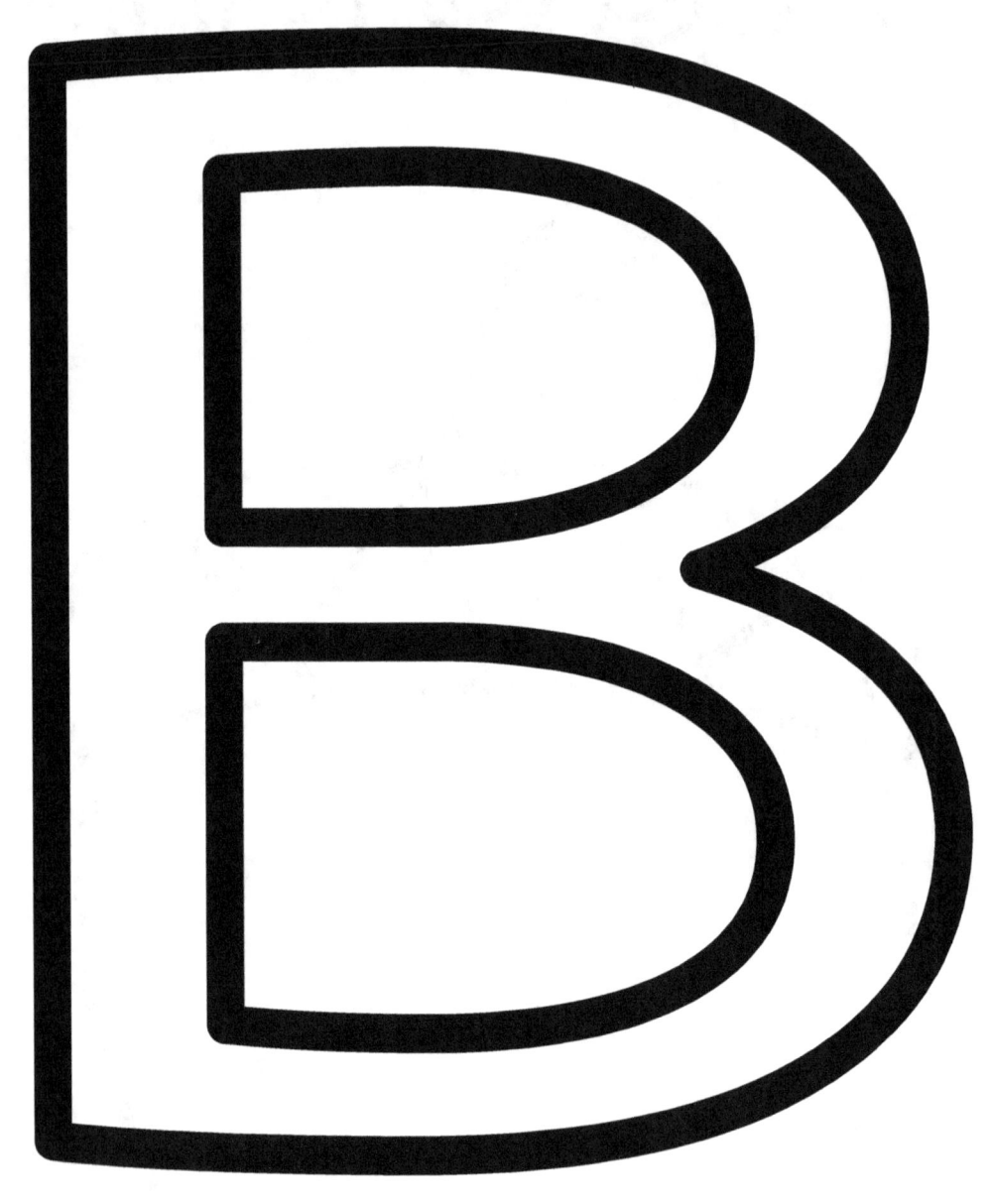

Balloons

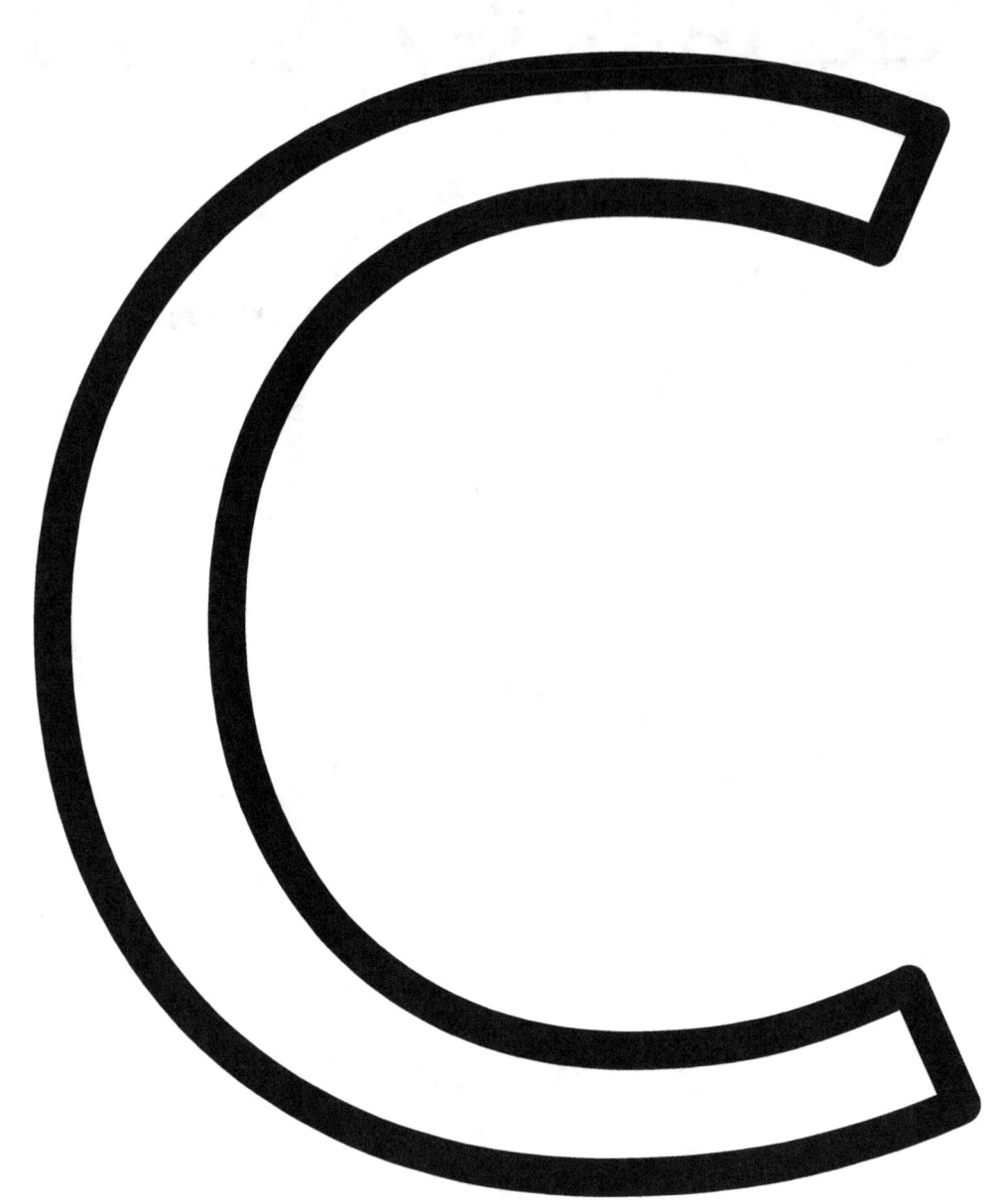

Cheese

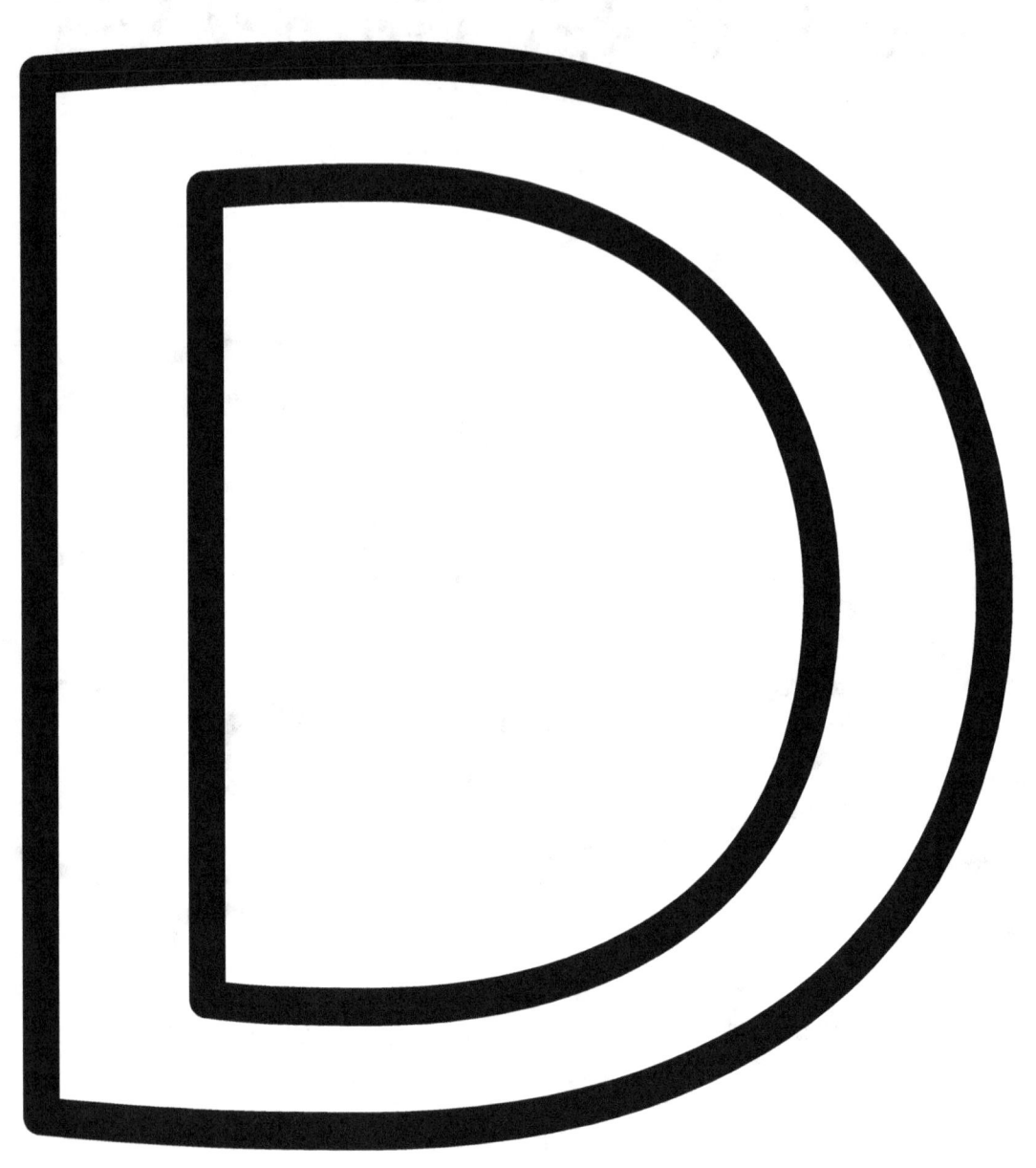

Drum

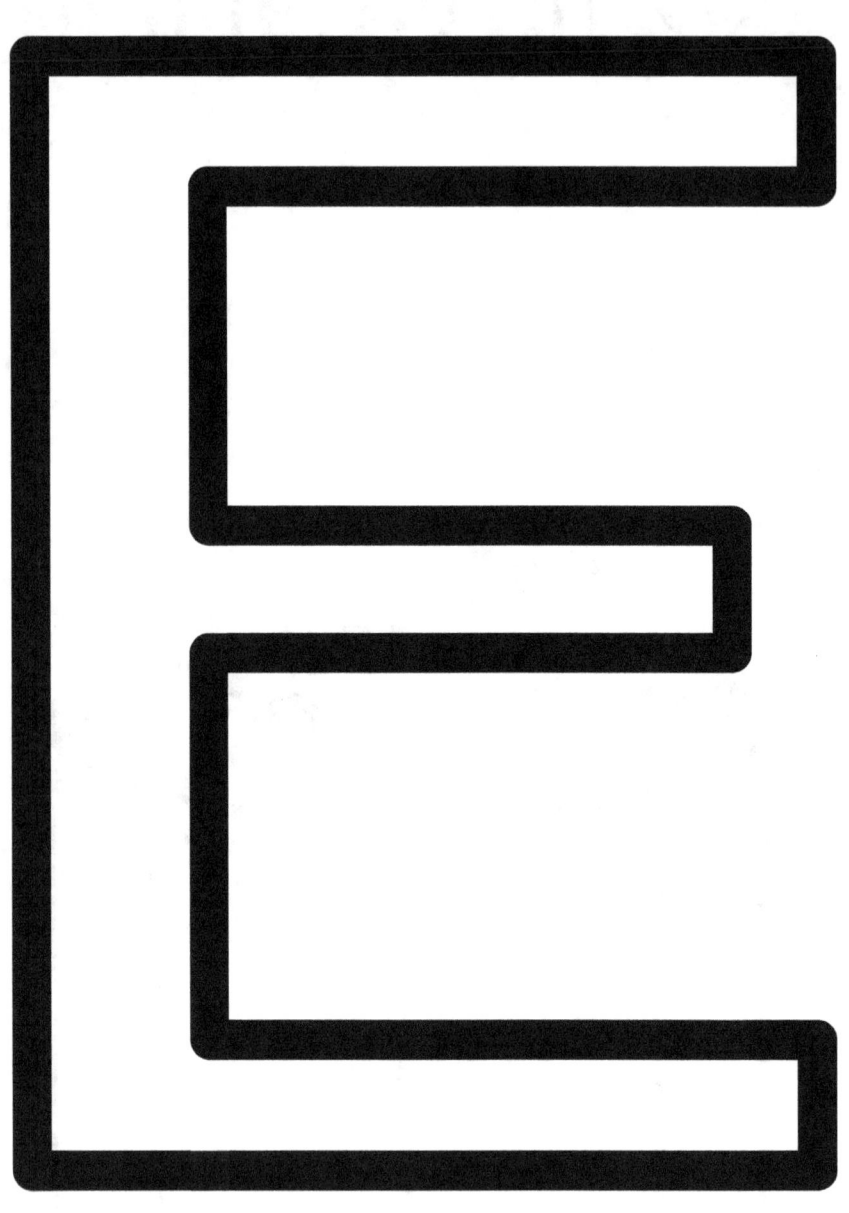

Eagle

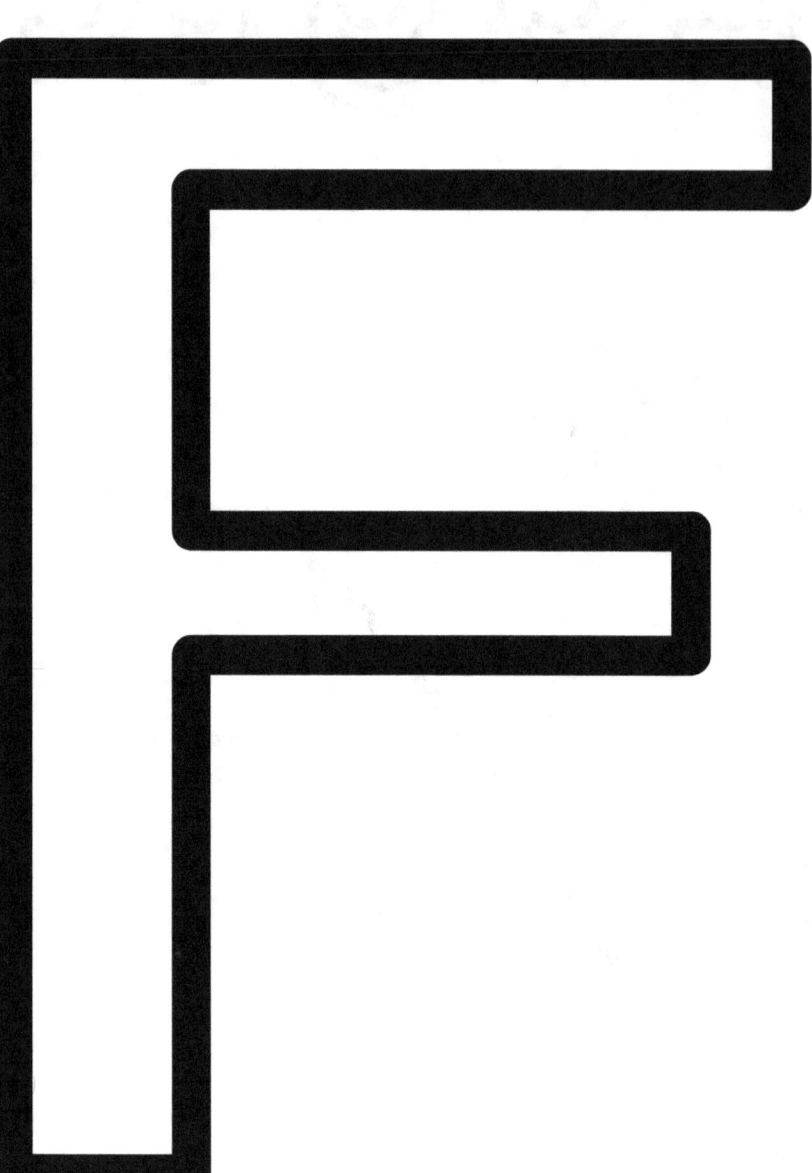

Fire

Guitar

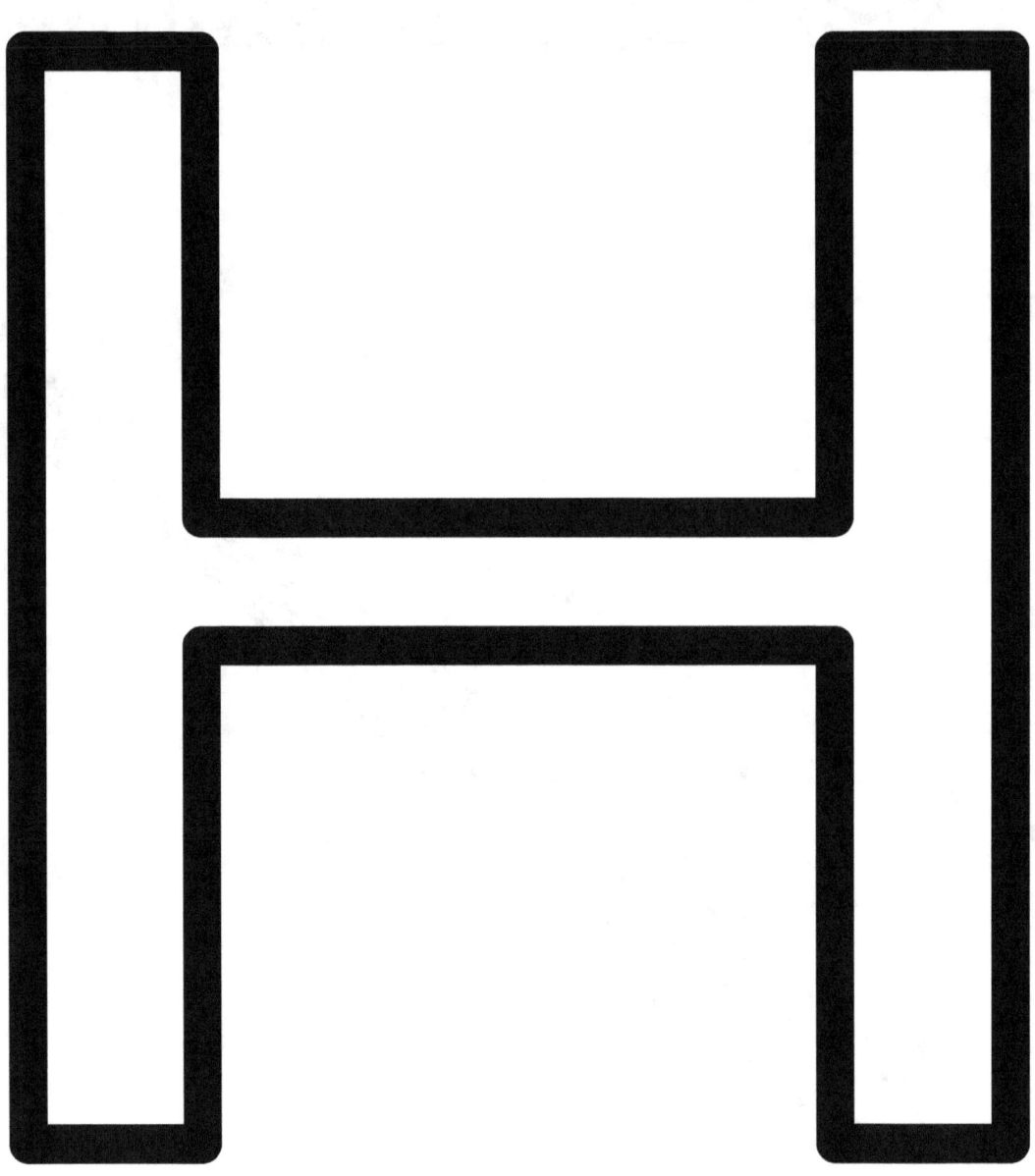

Hammer

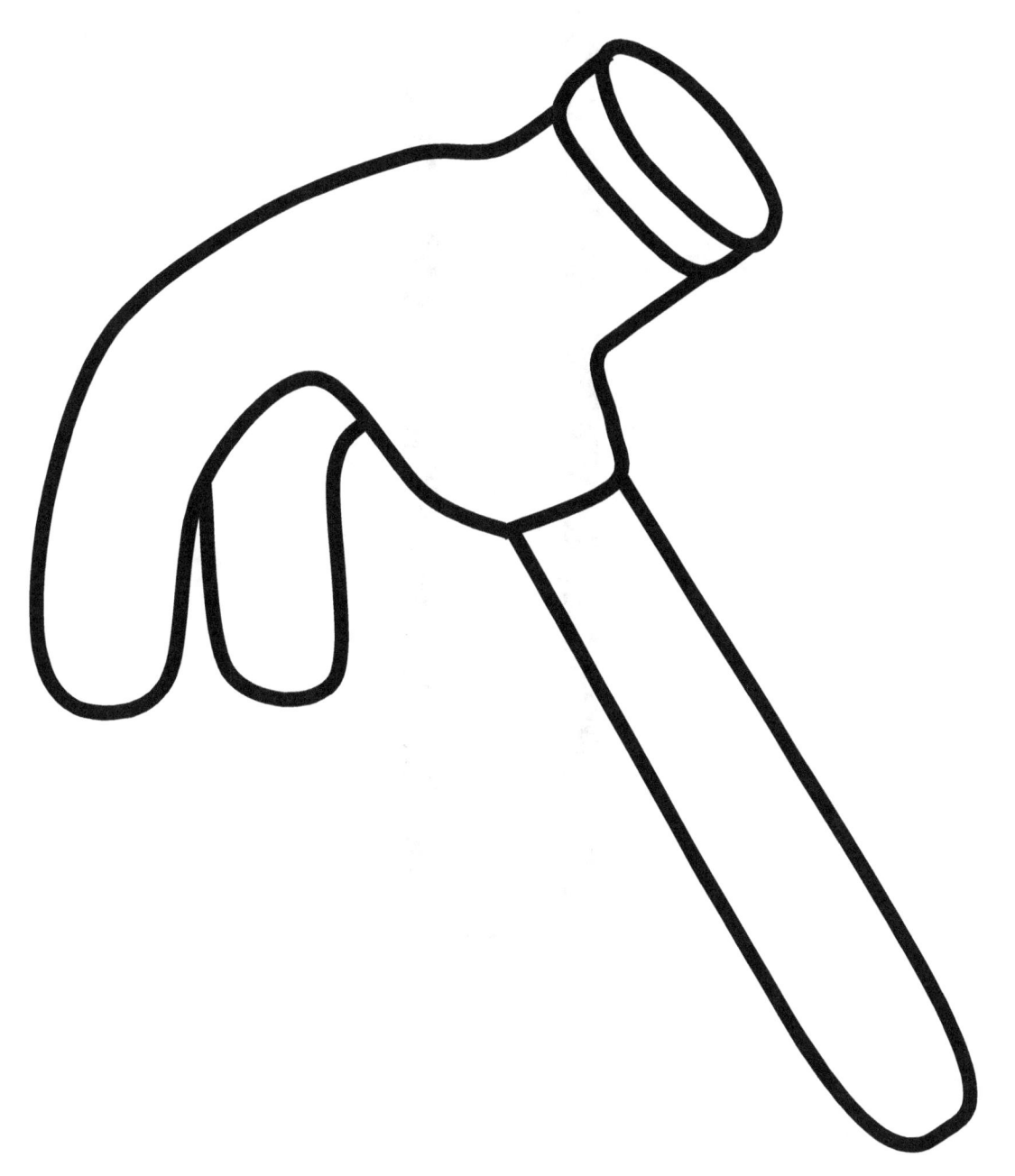

Iguana

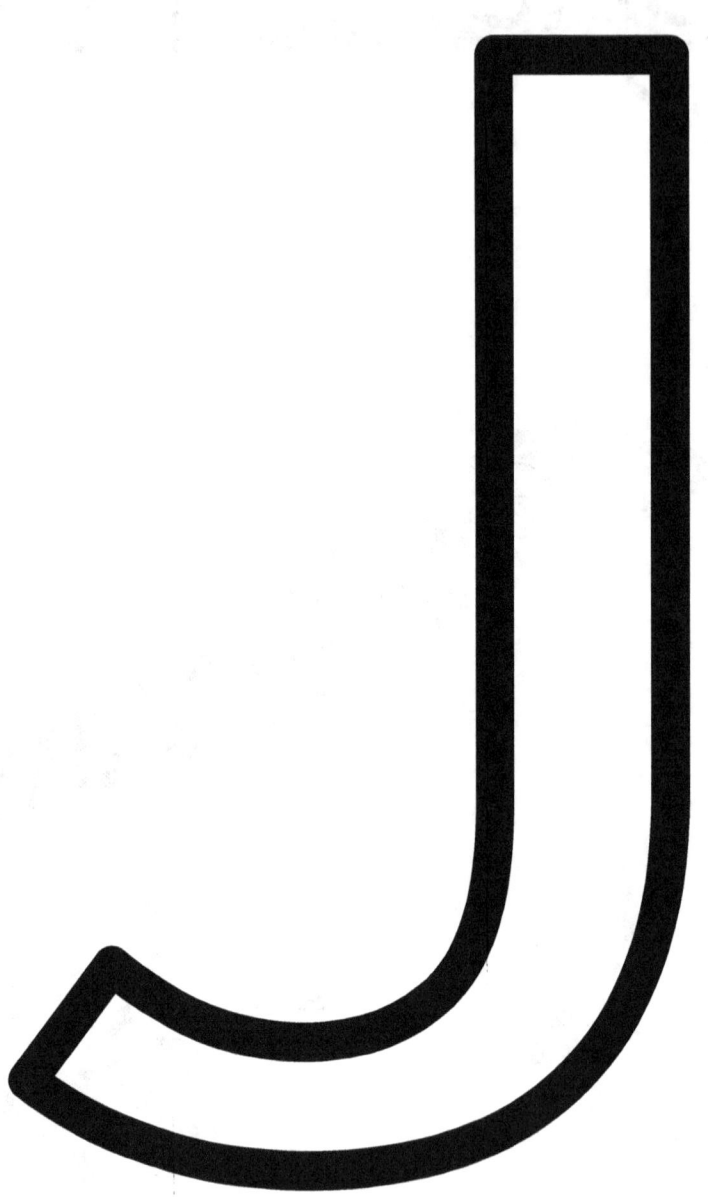

Jug

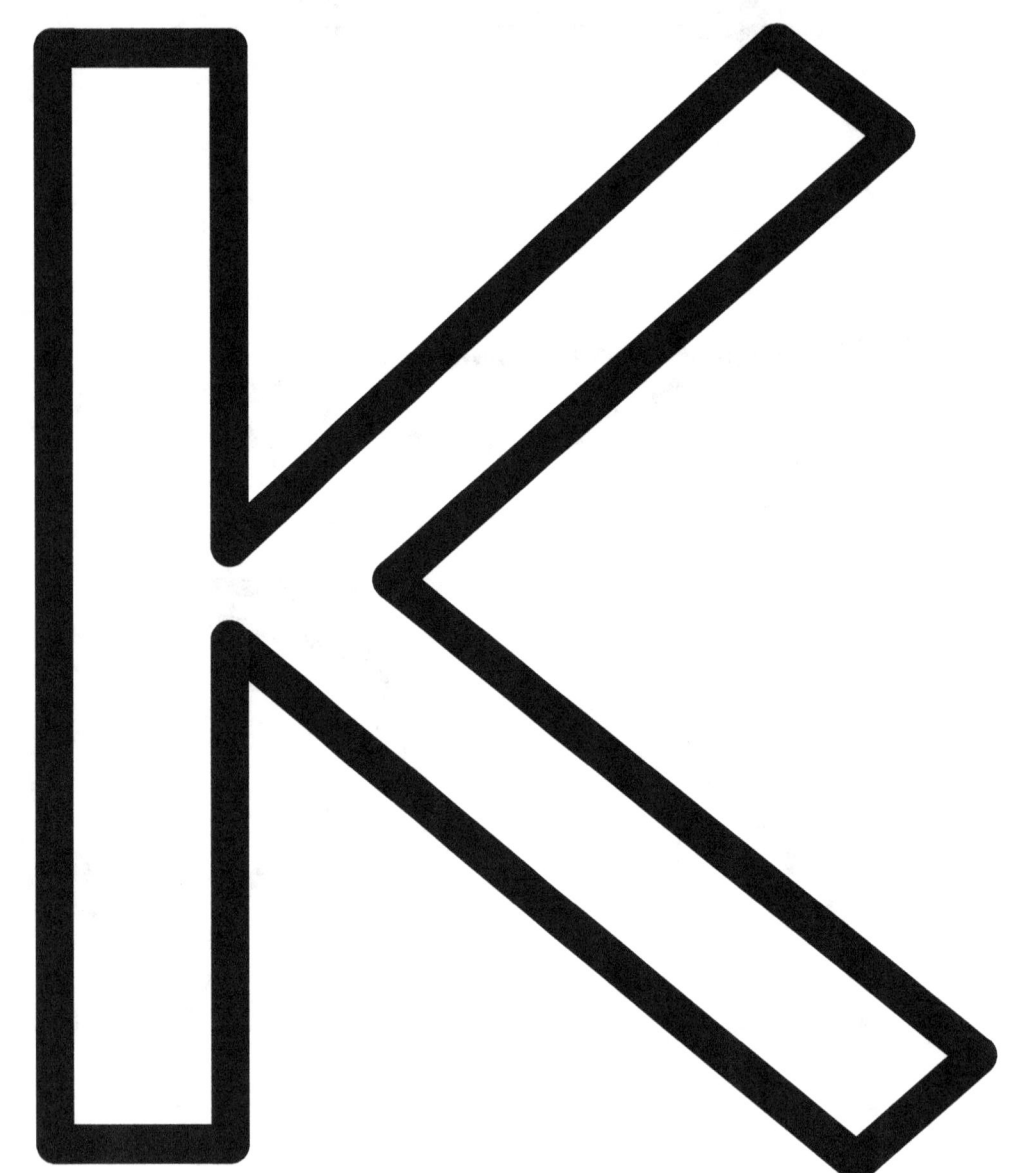

Kiwi

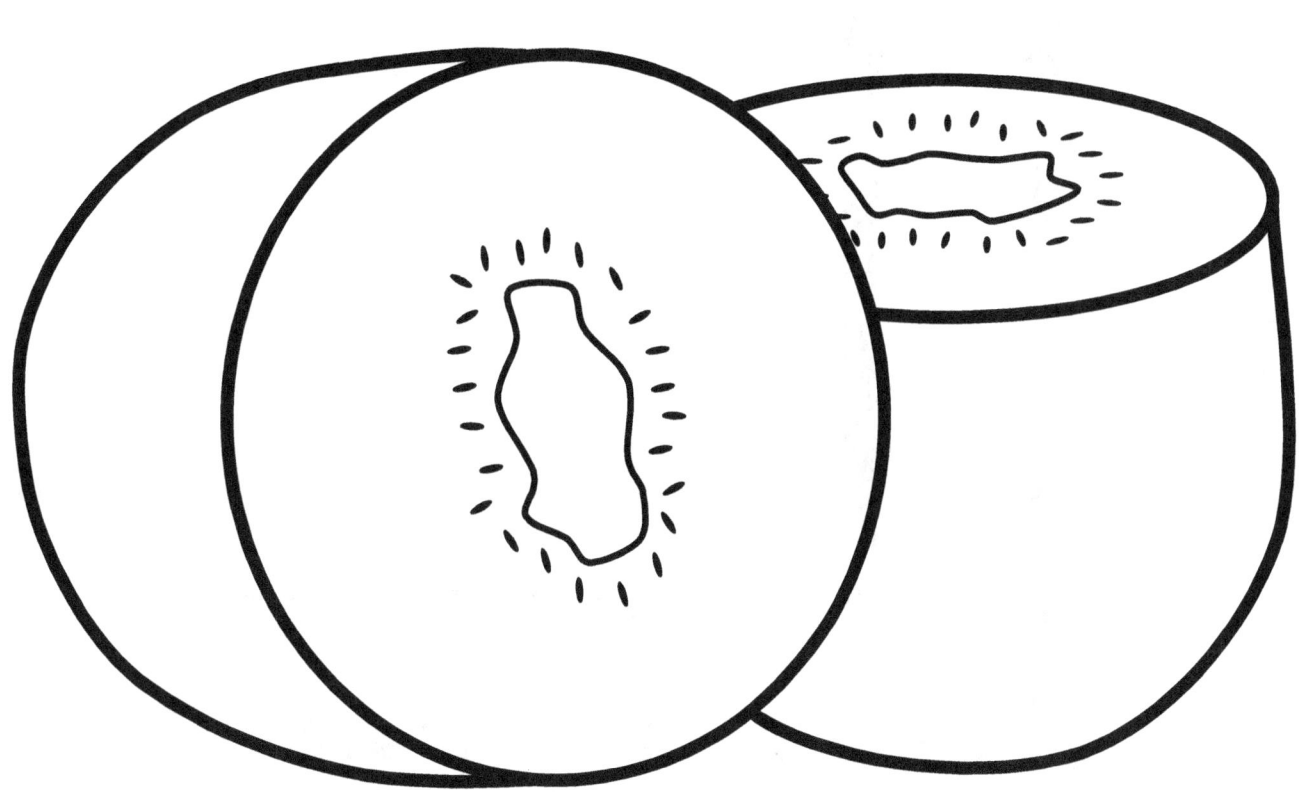

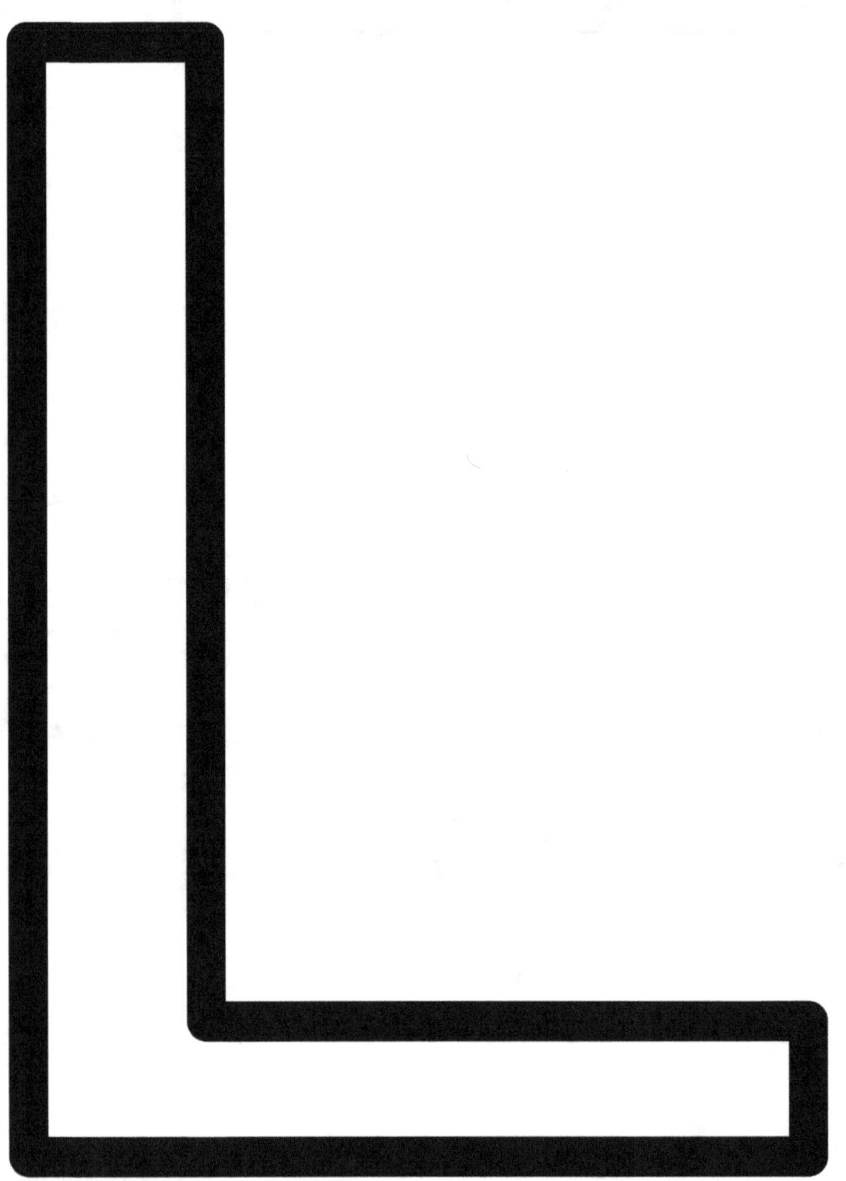

Ladybug

Milk

N

Necklace

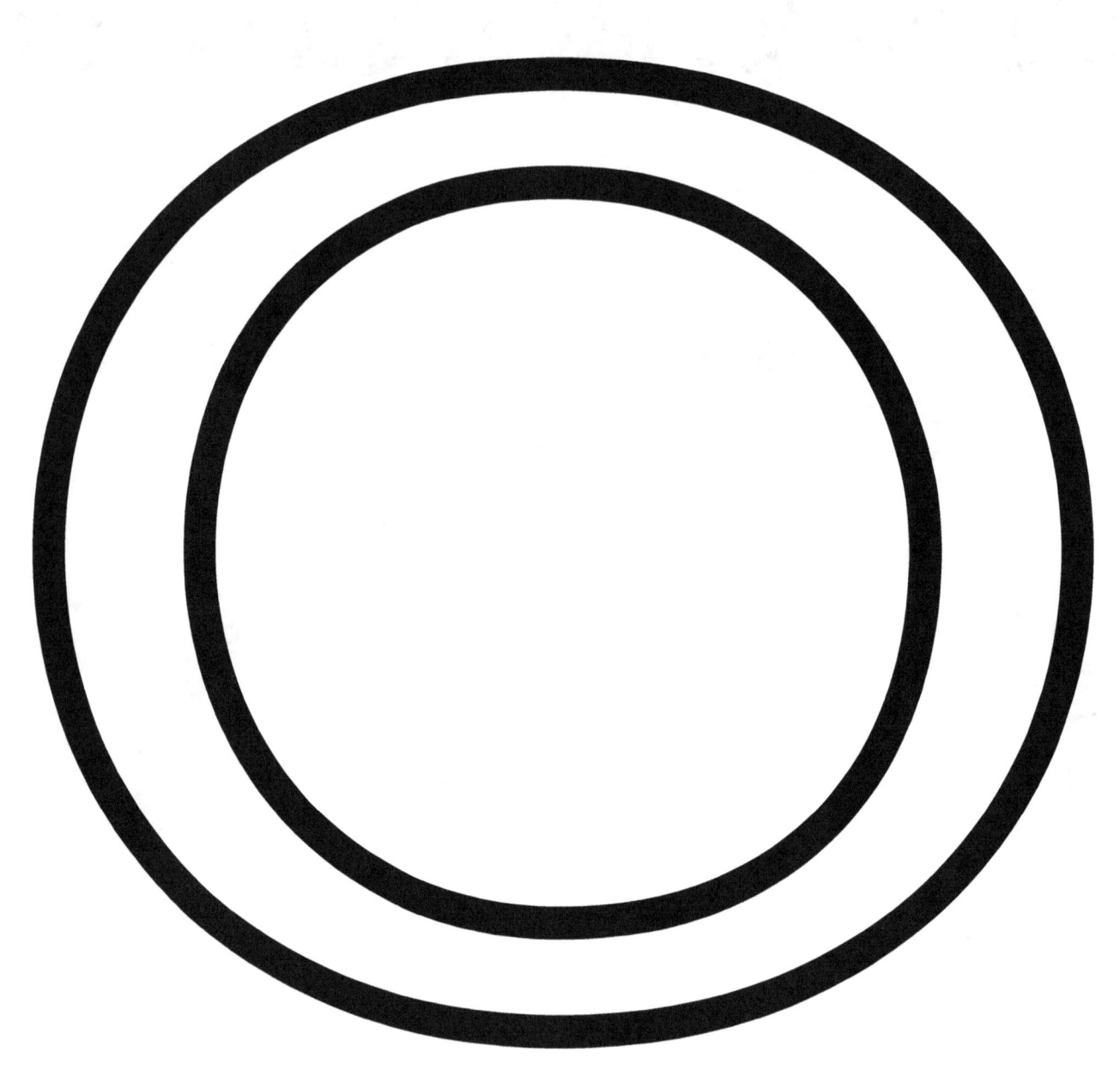

Oar

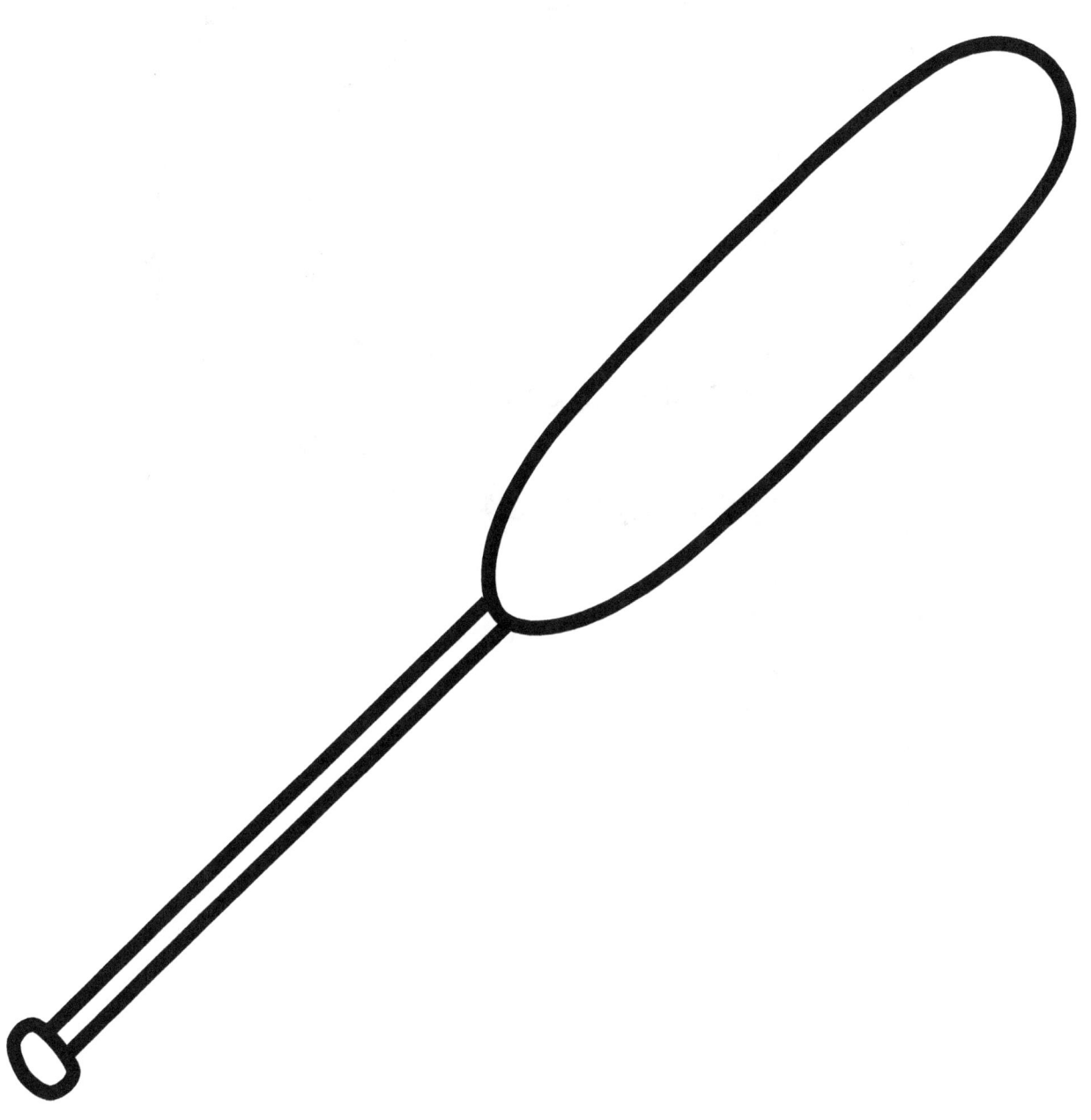

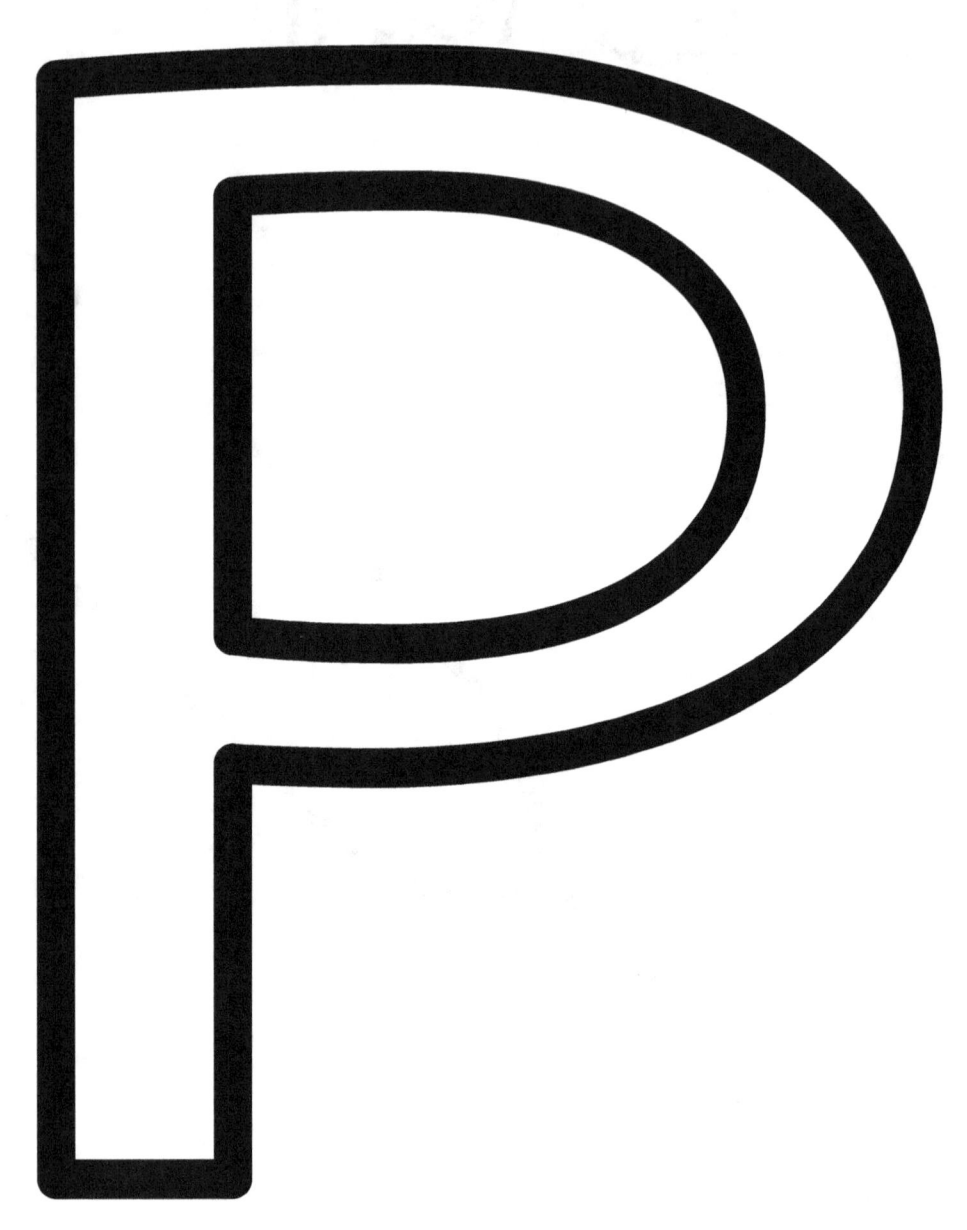

Phone

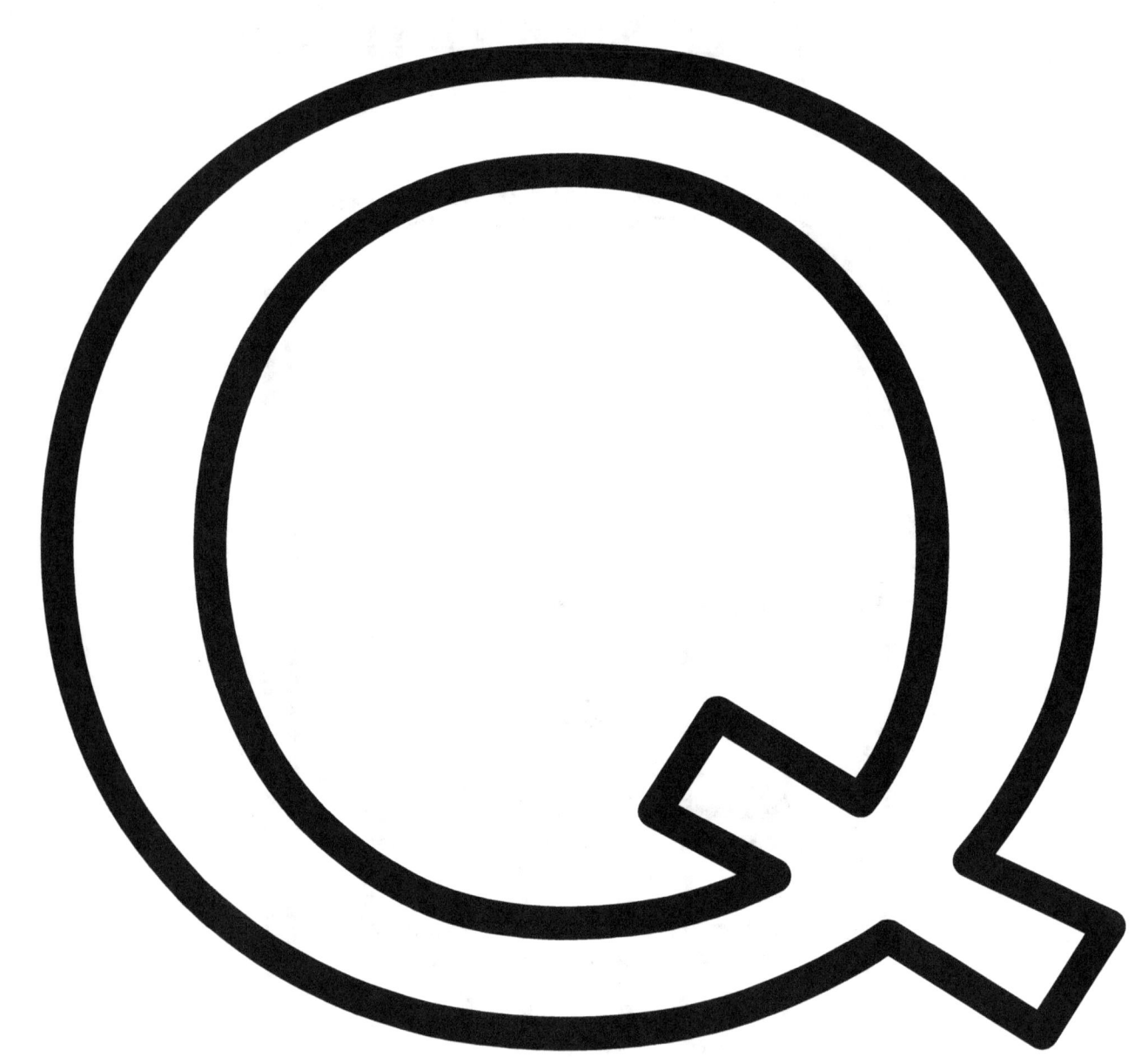

Quill

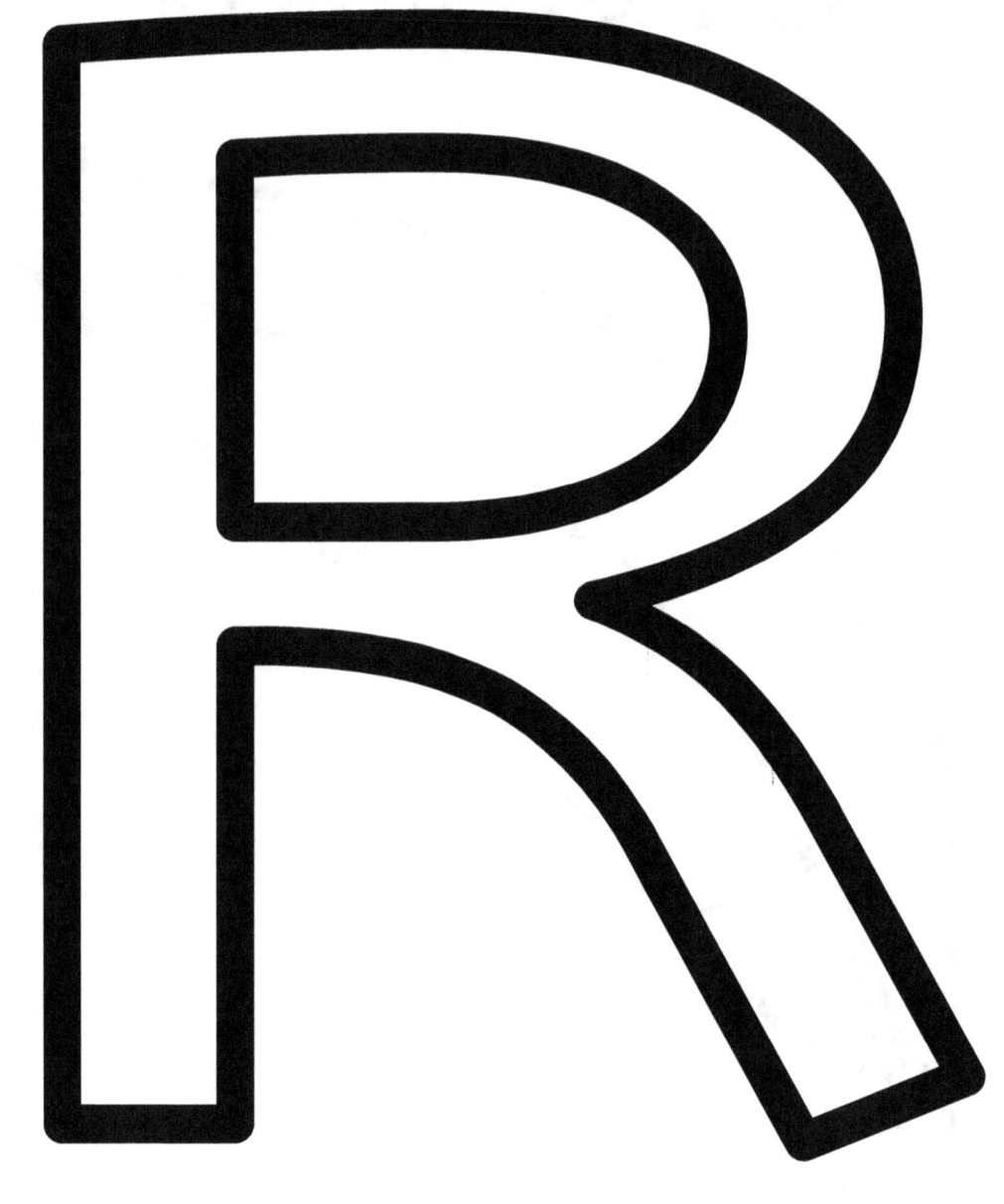

Robot

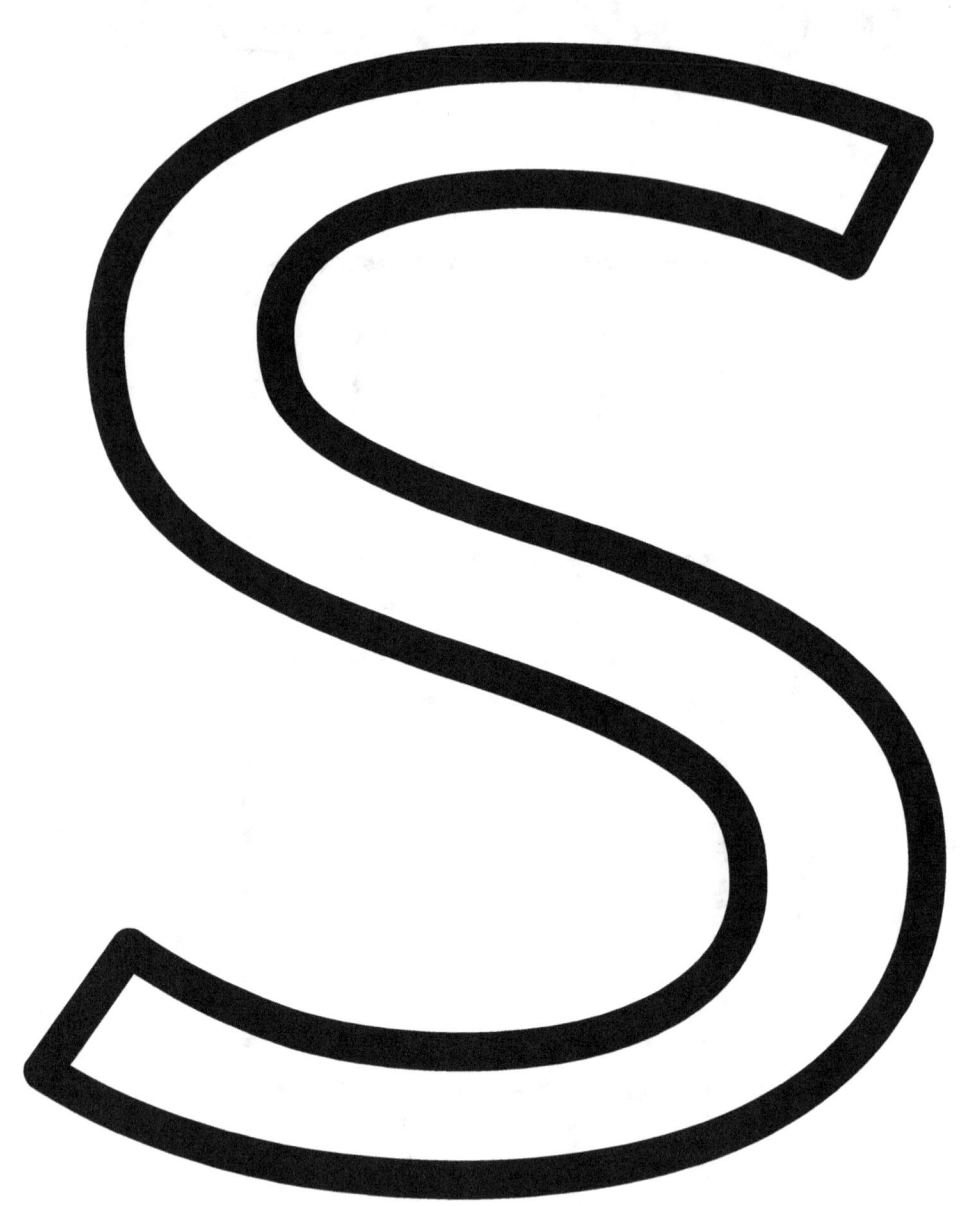

Sun

Tree

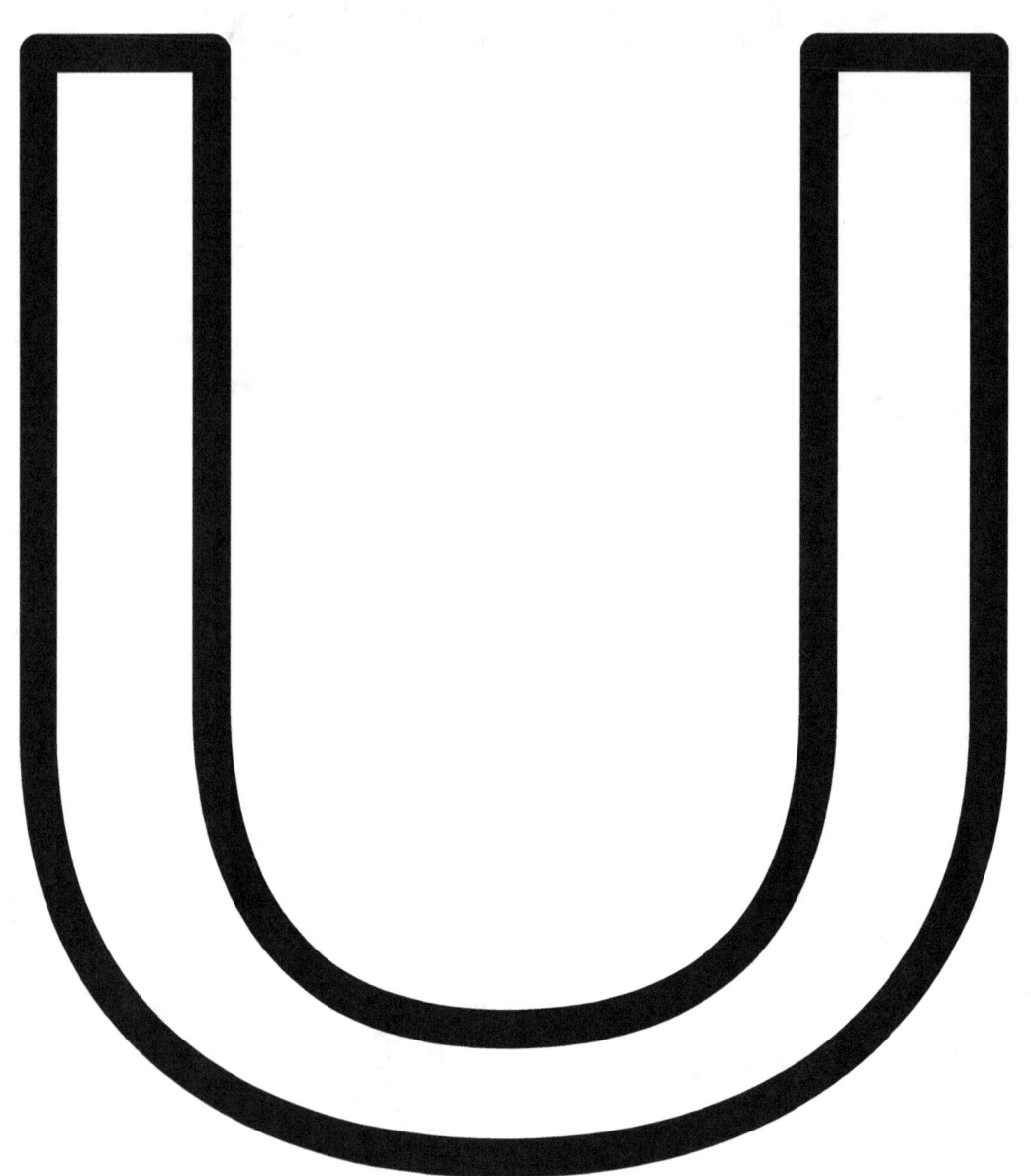

Umbrella

Vest

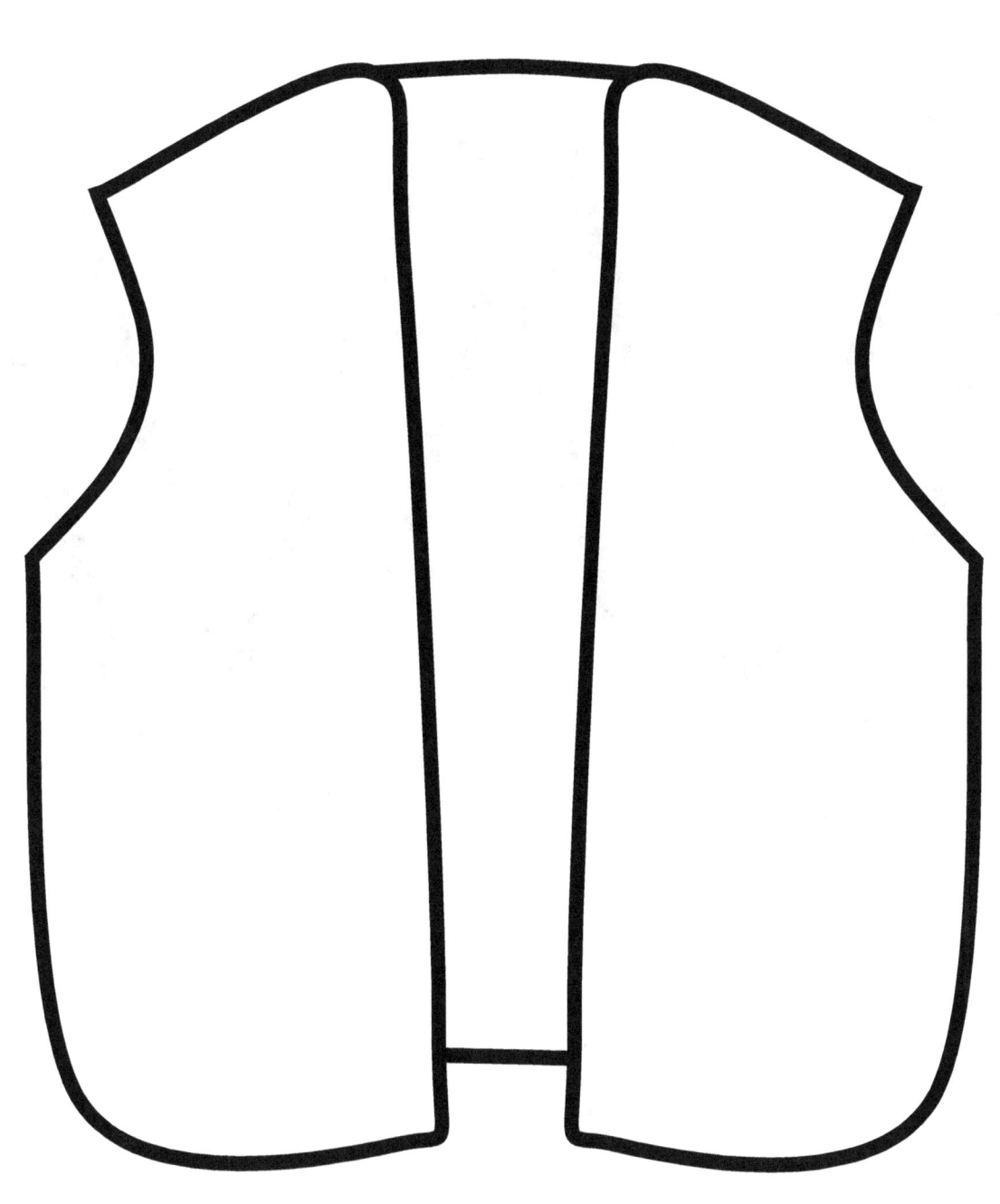

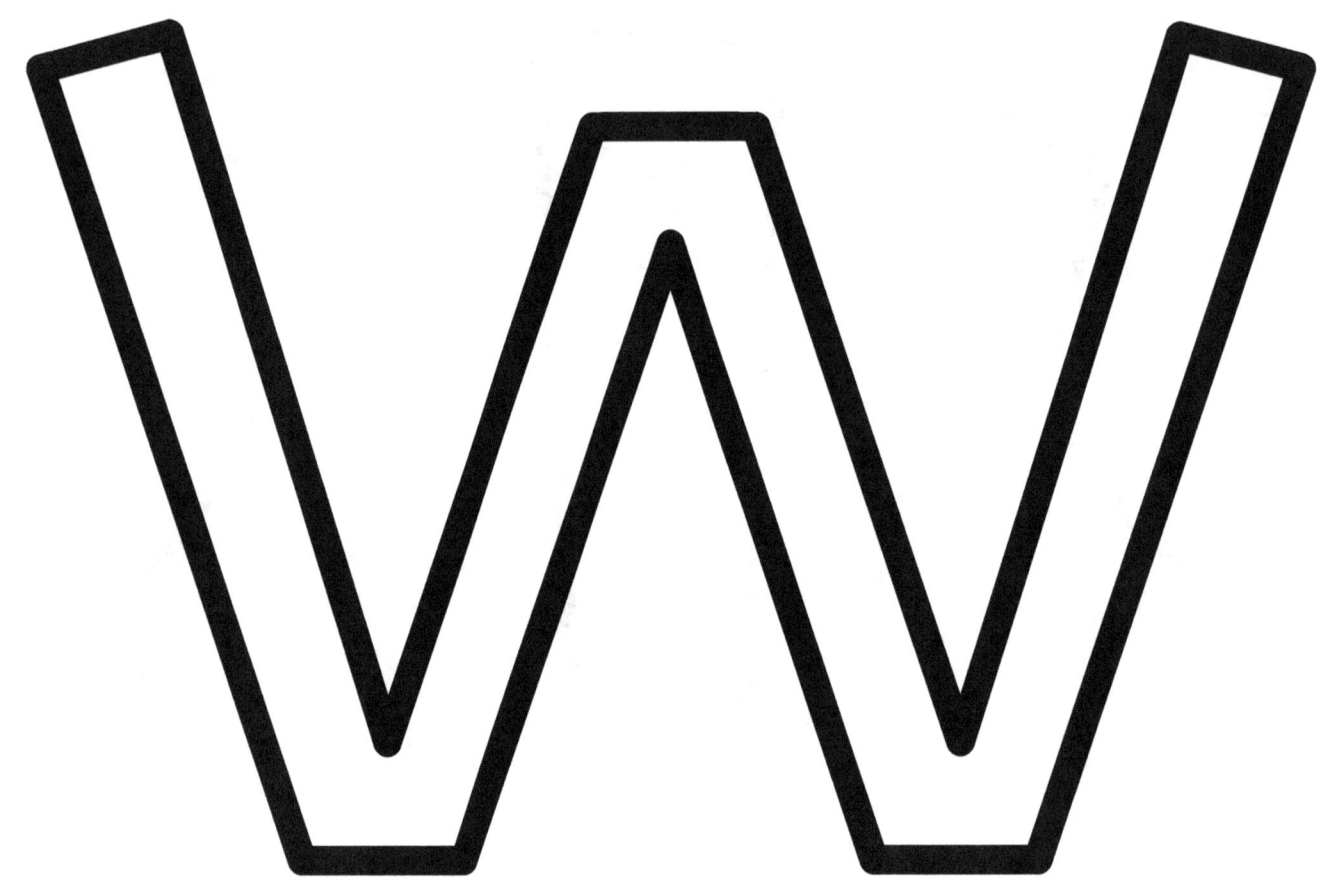

Watch

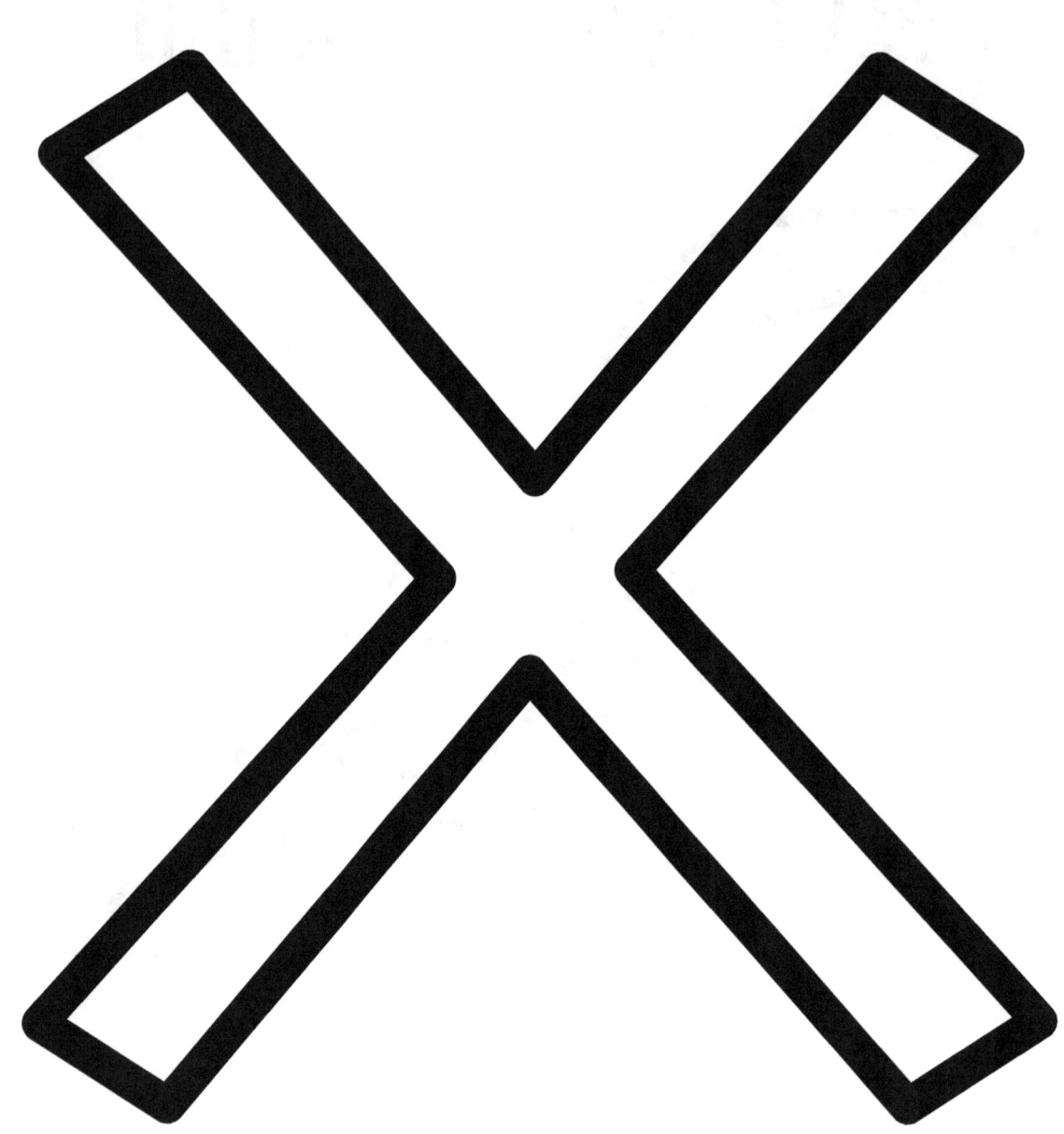

Xylophone

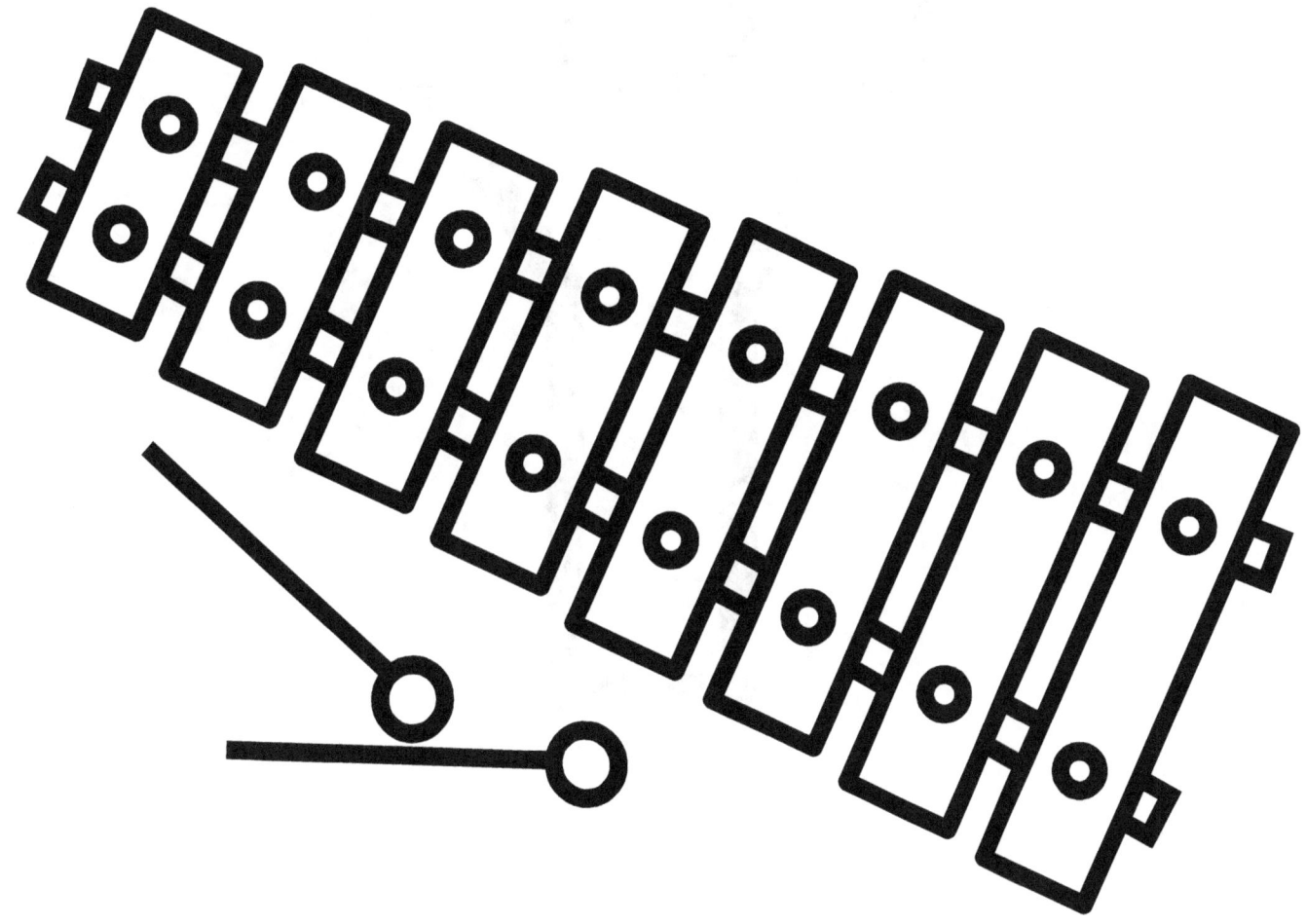

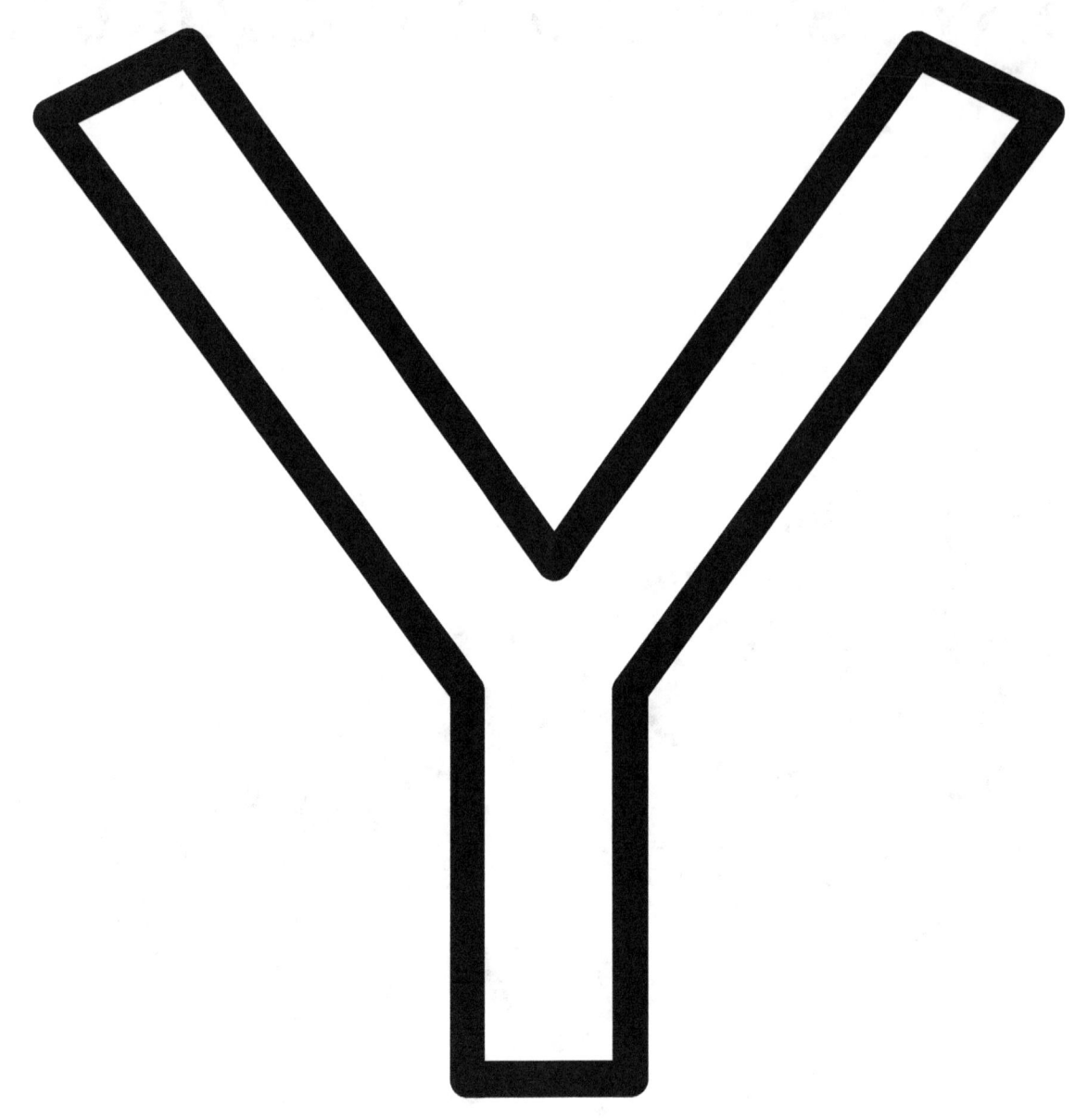

Yarn

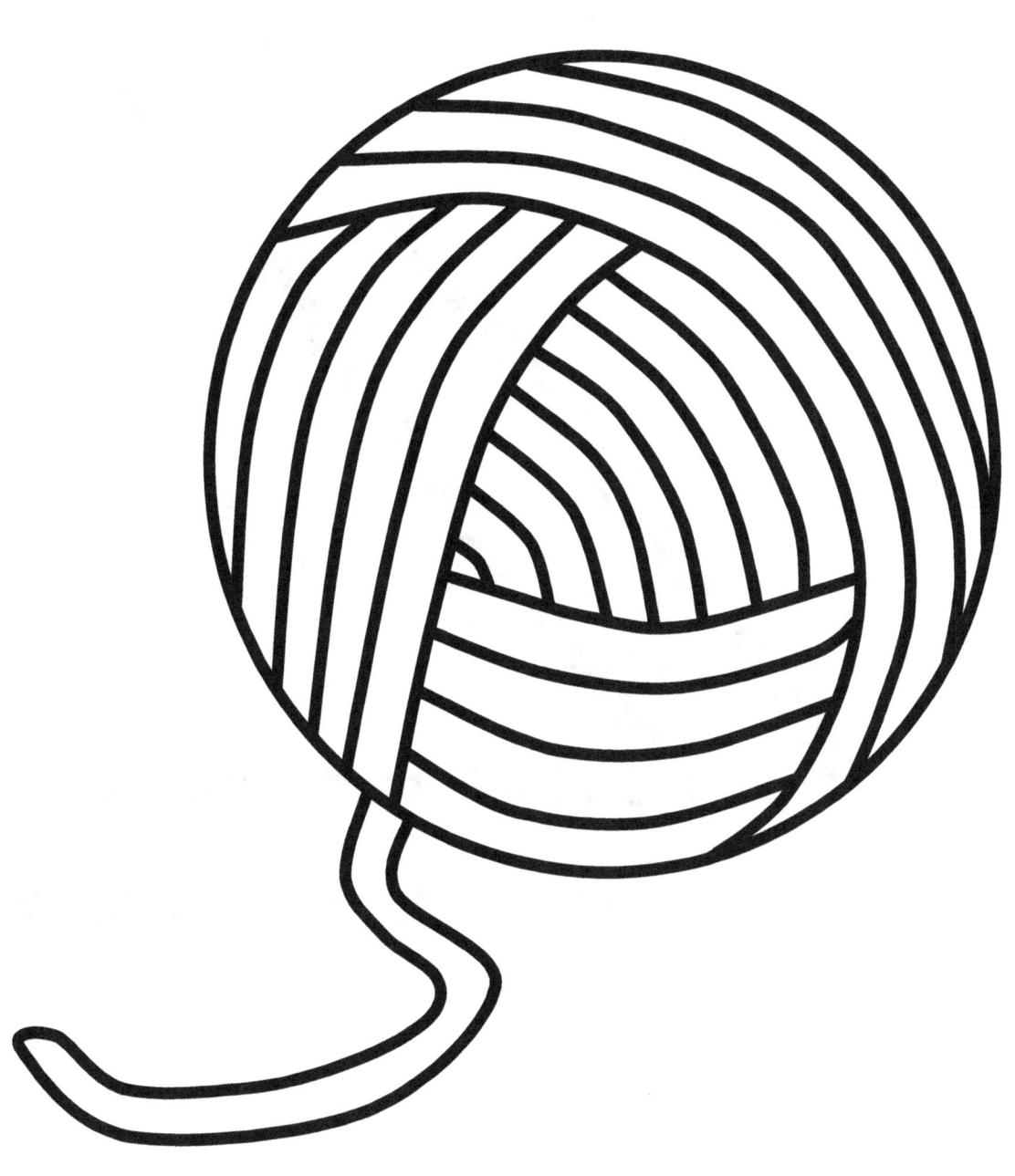

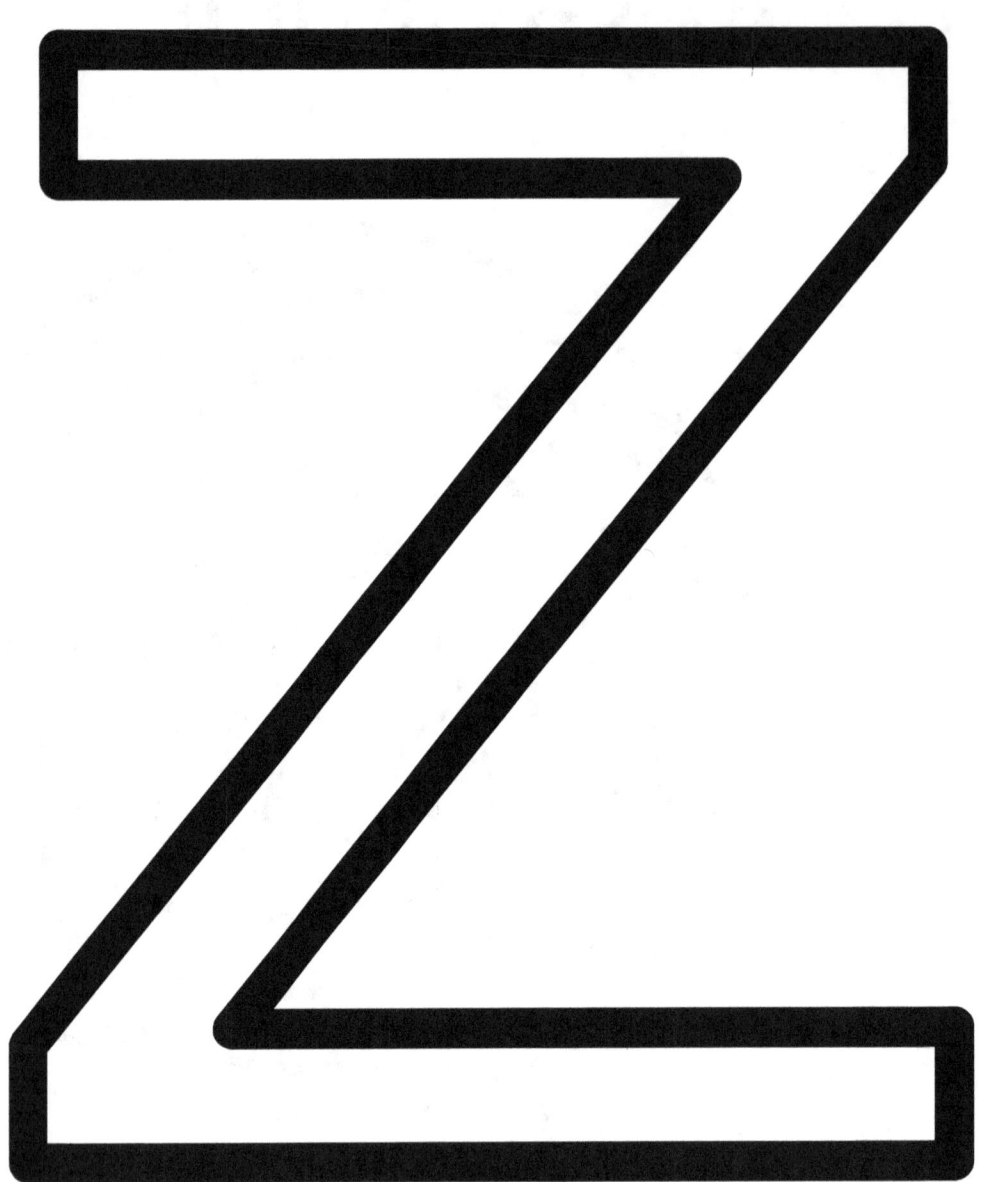

Zipper

Also by Sharon Asher